SURVIVOR STORIES™

SHIPWRECK

True Stories of Survival

Porterfield

rosen publishing's
rosen central®

New York

Published in 2007 by The Rosen Publishing Group, Inc.
29 East 21st Street, New York, NY 10010

First Edition

Library of Congress Cataloging-in-Publication Data

Porterfield, Jason.
Shipwreck : true stories of survival / Jason Porterfield.
p. cm. – (Survivor stories)
Includes bibliographical references and index.
ISBN-13: 978-1-4042-1000-4
ISBN-10: 1-4042-1000-8 (library binding)
1. Shipwrecks–Juvenile literature. 2. Survival after airplane accidents, shipwrecks, etc.–Juvenile literature. I. Title.
G525.P575 2006
910.4'52–dc22

2006023340

Printed in China

On the cover: The *Oceanos*, a Greek luxury liner, sinks off the coast of South Africa on August 4, 2001.

CONTENTS

The cargo ship *Secil Japan* sank off the coast of England on March 17, 1989. Despite advances in navigation technology, treacherous coastlines and unpredictable seas still sink ships piloted by even the best captains.

INTRODUCTION:
THE SHIP GOES DOWN

The ship *Neptune* was sailing across the North Atlantic in 1814 when the captain spotted what looked like a flag near the shore of a barren, uncharted island. He sent a crew out in a longboat to investigate. They returned with a ragged-looking man who wore clothes made of seal skins and clutched at a battered and notched oar.

The man was Daniel Foss, the sole survivor from the shipwreck of the *Negociator*, a brig that struck an iceberg and sank in 1809. Foss and two other men escaped in a lifeboat with some supplies, but only Foss made it to the island.

The island was barren of plant life and lacked fresh water. Foss drank rainwater that collected in hollows. For food, he killed seals and dried their meat in the sun. At other times, he ate fish that washed ashore during storms. To keep himself busy, he built a sturdy house out of stone, eventually adding a fence and a thirty-foot signal tower. His only tools were a small knife and an oar from his lifeboat. Each day, Foss cut a single notch in his oar. Nearly five years passed before he was rescued by the *Neptune*.

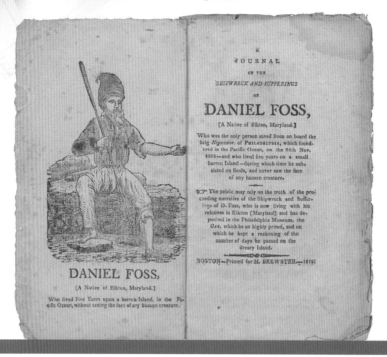

Daniel Foss published his own account of his ordeal in 1816, the year he returned to the United States. Foss is shown here holding his oar, which he eventually donated to the Philadelphia Museum.

Shipwrecks such as the one that sank the *Negociator* are hazards that seafarers have lived with since the beginning of sea travel. Over thousands of years, ship propulsion has evolved from sails and oars to steam and later to diesel and electricity, but the causes of shipwrecks have remained the same. Ships sink because they strike submerged objects or icebergs that knock holes in the hull, or they are buffeted by massive waves caused by storms. Mechanical failures, warfare, poor design, overcrowding, and human error can all be factors in causing a shipwreck.

Modern technology has made sea travel safer. Ships sailing in earlier eras had no way of knowing whether a fast-moving storm was coming. Before radio, they couldn't signal for help if they struck a remote reef. Today's thick steel hulls are much harder to penetrate than wooden hulls. Whereas sailors once relied exclusively on lighthouses, charts, and their own experience in navigating near shore, today, they use radar, sonar, and satellite technology to avoid reefs and other dangerous obstacles. In the past, the danger of remaining lost at sea was much higher, and the few people who survived, like Daniel Foss, had to endure harsh conditions over weeks, months, or even years.

Today, when ships meet with disaster, survivors can be reached with greater ease. The most dramatic tales of hardship and endurance took place in the distant past. Still, safety measures and modern technology cannot prevent every shipwreck. Tales of shipwreck survival remind us of the power of the seas, as well as the power of human endurance.

1

THE WHALE SHIP *ESSEX*

The whale ship *Essex* left the port city of Nantucket, Massachusetts, on August 12, 1819, on a two and a half year whaling expedition to the South Pacific. The *Essex* was a successful ship, one that spent twenty years bringing its share of whale tallow back to Nantucket to be rendered into lamp oil and other products. At 236 tons (214 metric tons) and 87 feet (26.5 meters) long, it sported twelve massive sails and carried three whale boats to help bring in harpooned whales.

Captain George Pollard was making his first trip as a captain. The ship's officers, First Mate Owen Chase and Second Mate Matthew Joy, were seasoned sailors. The twenty-man crew was an assortment of green and experienced whalers. The cabin boy, fourteen-year-old Thomas Nickerson, and his friends Barzillai Ray, Owen Coffin, and Charles Ramsdell, were all making their first voyage.

Whenever the ship's lookout sighted a whale, the crew lowered the whale boats and rowed out in pursuit. They maneuvered the boats as close as possible and speared the whale with barbed harpoons. When the whale tried to swim away, the whale boats pursued until it became

A crew of whalers prepares to harpoon a whale while the ship waits in the background. Adding to the perils of the seafaring life, the size and unpredictability of the whales made whaling a dangerous occupation.

exhausted. The whalers then killed the whale with a well-thrown lance and rowed it back to the ship where they would cut away its blubber and boil it down to oil. By the fall of 1820, the crew of the *Essex* had harpooned enough whales to make 700 barrels of valuable oil.

On November 20, 1820, the crew sighted yet another whale. They launched the three whale boats, commanded by Pollard, Chase, and Joy. The three boats latched on with their harpoons and towlines, leaving the *Essex* behind.

OWEN CHASE

Chase's whale boat was damaged in the pursuit. He and his crew of seven men were forced to row back to the *Essex* for repairs. They were hammering at the boat's stern when another whale surfaced just 100 feet (30.5 m) away from the ship. This whale was massive, estimated by Chase to be 85 feet (26 m) long. It was apparently

bothered by the sound of their hammering. Whales had been known to attack whale boats—a danger of which all whalers were aware—but one had never attacked a ship. Chase later said that he never guessed the whale would charge the ship until it began moving. The whale hit the ship with tremendous force, knocking Chase and his men to the deck. Before Chase could react, the whale circled and rammed the ship again, knocking a hole in the hull.

Owen Chase became a successful captain following his rescue. He was, however, plagued by persistent headaches.

Badly damaged, the ship began capsizing. When he saw

the hole, Chase ordered his men to grab any available supplies and to return the whale boat to the water. Within twenty-five minutes, he and his men were rowing away from the ship.

GEORGE POLLARD

Captain Pollard was stunned to discover that the *Essex* had capsized. After conferring with Chase and Joy, he decided that their only chance of survival would be to try to make it to South America, 2,000 miles (3,219 km) away. Pollard examined the supplies that Chase and his crew had brought from the stricken ship and saw at once that they were inadequate.

Looking at the ship through a telescope, he noted that supplies on one side had not gotten wet. Under Pollard's orders, the men cut the ship's masts and sails loose. With this weight suddenly removed, the ship righted itself. The crew boarded and salvaged food, water, and tools. Pollard calculated that the journey to South America would take fifty-six days. With careful rationing of the food and water, he and his men should have been able to make it to the coast of Chile or Peru.

The rationing worked well for the first month at sea. On December 20, they landed on tiny Henderson Island in the South Pacific Ocean. The men were tired and hungry, but not starving. They gorged themselves on fruit and wild game. Many wanted to stay and wait for rescue. Pollard, examining the island's resources, judged that there would not be enough food for all twenty men. Six days after their arrival, he and sixteen others stocked up on food and water and returned to the sea in another attempt to reach South America. Three men—Thomas Chappell, Seth Weeks, and William Wright—elected to stay on the island.

Things began to go wrong soon after the whale boats left the island. The three boats became separated from each other. The situation quickly disintegrated in Pollard's boat. Their food supply ran out on January 14, 1821. Six days later, sailor Charles Shorter died. Pollard realized that without food, the others would soon follow. He offered the men the choice of eating Shorter's body or dying themselves. Thereafter, they cannibalized their dead.

Eventually, only Pollard, his cousin Owen Coffin, Barzillai Ray, and Charles Ramsdell were left. When their gruesome supply of food ran out, the crew suggested that they draw lots and eat the loser. Worn down by their arguments, Pollard eventually consented. Lots were drawn, with Coffin selecting the shortest straw. The men killed and ate him. Ray died several days later and was also devoured. The ordeal ended on February 23, when the British ship *Dauphin* came across the whale boat. When Pollard and Ramsdell were rescued, they were found huddling at opposite ends of the boat, clutching gnawed human bones.

CABIN BOY THOMAS NICKERSON

Thomas Nickerson was the youngest and lowest-ranking member of the crew. His duties included menial cleaning tasks and lookout duty. A member of Chase's whaling crew, Nickerson was the first to sight the monstrous whale that attacked the ship. According to Nickerson, Chase passed up a chance to spear the whale as it moved alongside the ship, fearing that it might damage the ship's rudder.

Nickerson remained with Chase throughout the ordeal, from the sinking of the *Essex* to their eventual rescue. He had known Chase in Nantucket as a pleasant, friendly man. On board the *Essex*, he found Chase to be bullying and tyrannical. Over the three months spent in the lifeboat, he saw both sides of Chase. During the first weeks of the ordeal, Chase rationed the men's food and water at gunpoint. As their situation became desperate, he adjusted his manner and became more sympathetic. Nickerson marveled at Chase's ability to inspire the other men in the boat.

Two members of Chase's five-man crew died during the grueling experience. Nickerson, Chase, and Benjamin Lawrence survived. Nickerson gave much of the credit for their survival to Chase, who gave them tasks to distract them from their plight and helped them maintain hope. When their food supply ran out, they cannibalized the recently deceased Isaac Cole. The three men were finally rescued by the British ship *Indian* on February 18, 1821.

Thomas Nickerson, the *Essex's* cabin boy, was the first crew member to spot the attacking whale. During the ordeal in the lifeboats, Nickerson made several sketches to illustrate how the ship sank. Here he shows the whale charging the ship head-on.

RETURN TO LAND

The three men who had remained on Henderson Island survived and were finally picked up on April 5, 1821. Matthew Joy's boat, however, was lost at sea. In total, eight men survived the sinking of the *Essex* and the ordeal that followed.

The story of the *Essex* and its survivors caused a stir throughout the United States and abroad. The cannibalism horrified the public, but Nantucket and the seafaring community were quick to forgive the transgression. Even the death of Coffin was deemed legal when the desperate nature of the situation was taken into account. Seven of the eight survivors eventually returned to seafaring.

During his time in the whale boat, Owen Chase kept a detailed journal. A year after the sinking of the *Essex*, he published his account of the ordeal under the title *Narrative of the Most Extraordinary and Distressing Shipwreck of the Whale-Ship Essex*. A copy of the book eventually made its way into the hands of a young whaler named Herman Melville, who used it as the basis for his classic whaling epic, *Moby-Dick*.

2

THE *TITANIC*

On the night of April 14, 1912, the *Titanic* was four days into its maiden voyage across the Atlantic. With good weather and calm waters, the trip had gone smoothly for the 2,220 passengers and crew on board. There was even talk of the ship breaking a speed record, becoming the fastest ship to ever make the crossing from London to New York City.

The ship's journey ended at 11:45 that night when an iceberg suddenly loomed in front of it. The pilot saw it and tried to turn the ship away, but it was too late. The *Titanic* scraped alongside the iceberg, tearing a long gash in its side. The ship's hull began filling with water almost instantly. It sank in less than three hours, taking 1,523 passengers and crew to the bottom of the sea.

THE WORLD'S SAFEST SHIP

The *Titanic* was the latest ocean liner built for White Star Lines, a company that specialized in transatlantic travel. In those days before

The *Titanic* was the second completed ship of what was intended to be a trio of massive ocean liners built for White Star Lines. The other two ships were named the *Olympic* and the *Gigantic* to reflect their size.

passenger planes, anyone wanting to cross an ocean had to travel by ship. White Star prided itself on its safety record, the quality of its accommodations, its affordability, and the speed of its vessels.

For most passengers, speed and affordability were the most important factors. Many people making the voyage from Europe to America were emigrants hoping to find better lives in the United States. Companies like White Star Lines catered to both emigrants and sightseeing tourists. Wealthy passengers stayed in first class and received the best rooms, food, and entertainment; working-class and poor passengers occupied a much more cramped and basic third class; and middle-class passengers were put in second class, which fell somewhere between the other two.

With the *Titanic*, White Star Lines wanted to create the biggest and most luxurious ship ever seen. The ship was built with a capacity to hold 3,547 passengers and crew. Wide, sheltered promenades, a massive ballroom, and even a gym were all available for the wealthy. Even the third-class decks, located on the ship's lower regions, were supposedly as fine as second class on other ships.

In addition to deluxe accommodations, the *Titanic* was equipped with the latest safety features. Its hull was solid steel. Sixteen watertight compartments were built into the hull, designed to keep the ship afloat even in the unlikely event of the hull being breached. If water made it into the ship's lower decks, all of the doors to the higher decks could be shut automatically with the press of a button. A radio telegraph—the peak of communication technology—could signal other ships for help. Lastly, White Star Lines boasted that the *Titanic* had enough lifeboat seating for 1,178 passengers, far more than what was required by law.

In the end, the safety features did little good. The watertight compartments on the ship had been built with a head-on collision in mind. When the *Titanic* took a blow to the side, water simply rushed into the gash, filling the compartments and spilling over too-low bulkheads to flood other compartments. The lifeboats were wholly inadequate for the number of people on board the massive ship. The electronic locking system did nothing to stop the ship from sinking and served only to prevent passengers on the lower decks from reaching the upper decks and the lifeboats.

Ultimately, the safety features themselves may have given the passengers and crew a sense of overconfidence. There was no lifeboat drill before the *Titanic* left port. The passengers were not instructed on emergency procedures, and the crew was scarcely better prepared. Even after the ship hit the iceberg, many passengers reacted casually, dismissing the impact.

JOSEPH SCARROTT

Able Seaman Joseph Scarrott was thirty-three when he set sail to work on the *Titanic*. He had served on White Star ships before, but he didn't join the *Titanic*'s crew until four days before the departure date. When the order was given to abandon ship, Scarrott found himself in charge of lifeboat number fourteen. The *Titanic*'s officers ordered women and children into the boats first. According to Scarrott, some of the emigrant men who did not understand English tried to rush boat fourteen. Scarrott fought them back with the boat's tiller, throwing one man out of the boat three times. When he told Fifth Officer Harold Lowe what was happening, Lowe pulled out a pistol and fired two warning shots to discourage any further attempts.

Fifth Officer Harold Lowe, twenty-eight, was one of the youngest crew members on board the *Titanic* on the night the ship sank.

Boat fourteen was lowered into the ocean with fifty-four women, four children, two firemen, four stewards, and Scarrott and Lowe. Once in the water and away from the ship, Scarrott heard the *Titanic*'s boilers explode and watched the massive ship break in two and sink. With the help of Lowe and the other crew members, he guided the lifeboat among the dead, rescuing three survivors from the frigid water and eighteen others from a swamped lifeboat. Scarrott and Lowe then navigated their lifeboat through the icebergs to organize four other boats into a flotilla, tying them together until they were rescued that morning.

AMY STANLEY

Amy Stanley, twenty-four, was a third-class passenger aboard the *Titanic*, having left Oxfordshire, England, to take a job as a children's maid in the United States. She was in her room writing a postcard when the ship struck the iceberg. When she went out on deck to ask about the collision, a steward ordered her to return to her room. Instead, she fetched her roommates, American nurse Elizabeth Dowdell and her five-year-old charge, Virginia Emanuel. The women and child returned to the deck, where two men Stanley had befriended helped them into lifeboats.

Amy Stanley ended up in one of the four collapsible lifeboats. She and the thirty-eight others rowed the boat for several hours until the ship *Carpathia* picked them up. When the boat pulled alongside the *Carpathia*, Stanley fastened the rescue lines around the other women before being rescued herself. Once on board the ship, she was overjoyed to find that her two roommates from the *Titanic* had also survived.

Emily Ryerson

The Ryerson family of Pennsylvania, consisting of steel magnate Arthur, his wife, Emily, and their three children, were staying in first class when the collision occurred. Emily Ryerson was awake and heard the engines stop but did not feel the impact. She rang for a steward, who told her that the ship had slowed to avoid an iceberg. Ten minutes later, she looked out the cabin door and saw fellow passengers rushing to the deck wearing their life belts. She roused the rest of the family and led them onto the deck. Ms. Ryerson described the scene on the deck

Survivors row away from the sinking *Titanic*. The public outrage that followed the ship's sinking eventually led to laws requiring ships to provide lifeboats for everyone on board.

as calm, with Mr. Ryerson joking with other passengers and the ship's band still playing in the ballroom. Though reluctant to leave her husband, she took the children and boarded a lifeboat.

As it was lowered into the water, Ryerson could see water rushing into the *Titanic's* lower portholes. She watched as the ship's lights went out. She joined the others in rowing the boat away from the sinking ship. Her boat drifted aimlessly without a light until Fifth Officer Lowe located it and tied it to four others. Together, the five boats drifted among the ice until rescued by the *Carpathia*. Though Ryerson and her children survived, her husband went down with the ship.

AFTER THE ACCIDENT

The *Titanic*'s sinking provoked horror and outrage on both sides of the Atlantic. White Star Lines was faulted for not having enough lifeboats on board for everyone. Survivors blamed the crew for being

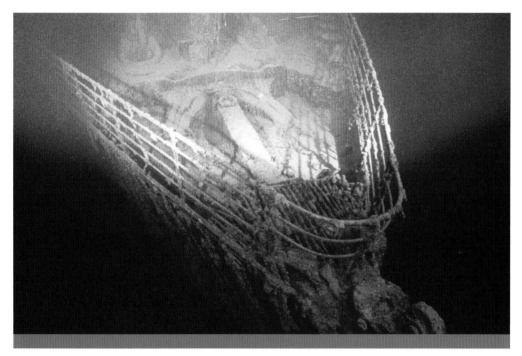

On September 1, 1985, a crew of explorers led by Robert Ballard and Jean-Louis Michel located the *Titanic*'s remains in roughly 12,000 feet (3,700 meters) of water off the coast of Newfoundland.

disorganized and giving preferential treatment to first-class passengers. Crew members accused passengers—particularly third-class passengers—of mobbing the lifeboats. Newspapers criticized the ship's builders for design flaws. Captain Edward Smith, who went down with the ship, was blamed for emphasizing speed over caution in waters prone to icebergs.

The sinking of the *Titanic* remains one of the worst maritime disasters in history and has been the subject of numerous books and movies. In 1985, a team led by Jean-Louis Michel and Robert Ballard located the wreck of the *Titanic* on the bottom of the Atlantic. Their photos of the wreckage reawakened public interest in the disaster. The ship remains where they found it, a monument to those lost in the tragedy.

3

THE *ENDURANCE*

On December 5, 1914, the *Endurance* set off from South Georgia, an island at the tip of South America, on one of the most daring expeditions ever undertaken. It was led by Sir Ernest Shackleton, the Antarctic explorer knighted for his achievements. He had spent years planning and preparing for the Imperial Trans-Antarctic Expedition. The *Endurance* would cross the Weddell Sea and land on the Antarctic continent. Shackleton and a team of men would then embark on an 1,800-mile (2,897 km) journey across Antarctica—on foot.

Twenty-eight men made up the expedition. A few, like officer Thomas Crean, had already served on previous Antarctic expeditions. In addition to the ship's crew, the members included two doctors, a photographer, an "official artist," and a team of scientists. They would conduct research in the Antarctic after Shackleton departed. There was even a stowaway. Eighteen-year-old Perce Blackboro had concealed himself on the ship with the help of three sailors. When he came out of hiding, Shackleton put him to work in the galley.

Shackleton expected the *Endurance* to reach Antarctica by the end of the month, the beginning of the Antarctic summer. But on December 8, the *Endurance* entered a section of polar pack ice. From then on, it was slow going. Although there were a few stretches of clear travel, most days were spent weaving and ramming through the smaller floes while avoiding heavy ice that could damage the ship.

On January 16, 1915, a blizzard forced the *Endurance* to take shelter on the protected side of a massive iceberg. When the ship resumed sail two days later, it made tortuously slow progress. Shackleton decided to stop again on January 19, hoping that the pack would open up once the blizzard had completely abated.

His hope was in vain. By January 24, the *Endurance* was frozen firmly in the pack and there was no clear water in sight. A month later, Shackleton finally admitted that there was no chance of escape from the ice before winter set in.

STRANDED!

The men ceased their routines and converted the *Endurance* into a winter station. They built "dogloos" out of ice and snow for the sled dogs that had been brought along for the expedition. They hunted seals and penguins, played games such as hockey and cards, and wrote in their diaries. Everyone kept their spirits up by thinking of the day that the ship would break free of the ice and resume its journey.

This photograph shows the *Endurance* beset by ice. Built by the renowned Framnaes shipyard in Norway, the *Endurance* was one of the strongest wooden ships ever constructed.

Even though the *Endurance* was frozen in place, wind and currents slowly carried the pack ice northward. As the dark winter ended, the pack broke up into massive fragments. These frequently collided, applying huge amounts of pressure. Everyone feared that such pressure would crush the *Endurance*. Beginning in August, the ship would occasionally rock and groan from the movement of the surrounding ice.

On October 23, their worst nightmare began to come true. Three floes converged to exert pressure on the *Endurance*. The ship began leaking, and the crew frantically pumped out the water. The next three days were exhausting and heartbreaking. Cracks gaped open between the planks of the *Endurance*. Its timbers splintered and snapped with the noise of gunshots. On October 27, at 5:00 PM, Shackleton gave the order to abandon ship.

The men set up camp on a floe 200 yards (183 m) from the *Endurance*. During the night, a crack opened up between the tents and they had to move to the other half of the floe. Two days later, they set out on a march to the northwest, dragging the lifeboats behind them. The plan was to make their way across the ice and ocean to Paulet Island off the Antarctic coast, where there was a stash of provisions.

It was grueling work. A few men scouted ahead of the main party and tried to clear a path through rugged ridges. The heavy boats sank deep into the snow. They averaged less than a mile of progress each day—and it was more than 300 miles (483 km) to Paulet Island. Before a week had passed, Shackleton gave the order to halt and set up camp.

They were still within easy distance of the wreck of the *Endurance*. Teams made several salvage trips for gear and provisions. On November 23, the men watched from the camp as the *Endurance* finally disappeared beneath the ice. A month later, another attempted march ended in failure.

The ice continued to drift northward. On March 23, 1916, Shackleton spied land off in the distance. It was the tiny Joinville Island, only 42 miles (67.6 km) away, but still beyond reach.

Throughout the time on the ice, food was a constant concern. Provisions from the ship were tightly rationed. The men began to rely on seal and penguin for meat as well as for blubber, which they used for fuel. In February and March, the shortage twice neared a crisis point. The men were forced to rummage through the refuse heap for edible scraps. They also had to shoot the dogs.

EXODUS BY LIFEBOAT

Toward the end of the month, the pack began to break apart. Huge chunks split off their floe, now bobbing in open water. On April 9, Shackleton gave orders to pack up and launch the lifeboats. He hoped to reach one of the islands to the west. After three days Frank Worsley, captain of the *Endurance*, checked their position. Due to an undetected strong current, they were actually 22 miles (35.4 km) farther from land than they were when they had left camp.

After being rejected as a sailor on the *Endurance* because of his age, Perce Blackboro stowed away aboard the ship.

Cold temperatures, soaked and frozen clothing, thirst, and lack of sleep began to take a toll on the men. A turn at the oars provided a brief respite, since it was the only way to keep active and warm. Many of the party suffered from frostbite and raw skin. Blackboro's feet were so badly frostbitten that he lost all circulation in them.

On April 14, the men were overjoyed to wake and find land dead ahead. When they landed, Shackleton decided to give Blackboro the honor of being the first man ever to set foot on the island. He gave the lad a hand over the side of the boat, and Blackboro tumbled to the ground. His feet were too damaged to hold him. Another man had a heart attack soon after reaching land.

They were on desolate Elephant Island off the Antarctic coast. There was no possibility that they would be discovered by a passing ship. Shackleton wasted no time. Ten days after landing, he chose five other men and set out again on the largest lifeboat, the *James Caird*. Their destination was South Georgia, 800 miles (1,287.5 km) away.

RESCUE AT LAST

Shackleton knew his chances of reaching his destination were remote. The *Caird* was traversing one of the most dreaded stretches of ocean on the globe. After threading their way through ice floes—any one of which could have shattered the *Caird*—the crew faced the open water and 50-foot (15.2 m) waves. Gales in the region could reach more than 150 miles per hour (241.4 kilometers per hour). The men awoke one morning to find that the boat was encased in a thick coating of ice,

The 1914 expedition was Sir Ernest Shackleton's third journey to Antarctica. No one questioned his leadership throughout the ordeal of the *Endurance*.

which periodically had to be chipped away by axe. Worse, the sea anchor broke away during a gale, making it much more difficult to control the boat. Two weeks into their long journey, they discovered that their second barrel of water was brackish.

On May 8, they glimpsed the cliffs of South Georgia. The water was so rough that the *Caird* could not make a landing until May 10. But the ordeal was not over. Between their camp and the whaling station lay

17 miles (27.4 km) of mountainous terrain regarded as impassable. After resting a few days to regain their strength, Shackleton, Worsley, and Crean set out on foot for the whaling station. They packed light and completed the entire harrowing journey in thirty-eight hours. Shackleton feared that if they stopped to camp, they would freeze to death. When they staggered into the whaling station on the afternoon of May 20, ragged and filthy, the whalers were awestruck.

Shackleton's most pressing concern was the rescue of the men still stranded on Elephant Island. Over the next few months, he attempted three rescue missions on three different vessels. Each time, the pack ice turned him away. When he set out a fourth time, on August 3, he was growing desperate.

Meanwhile, the men on Elephant Island were also losing hope. Elephant Island was a barren and hostile place prone to ferocious winds and blizzards. The men were forced to spend most of their time in improvised shelters made up of the boats, rocks, and wood scraps. The two doctors had to amputate Blackboro's toes on one foot. Their food supplies were almost exhausted.

On August 30, Shackleton's ship came into sight. The men over-turned their meager pot of shellfish and seaweed in their haste to reach the beach. One of the doctors hoisted Blackboro to his shoulders. Within the hour, they were all watching Elephant Island recede in the distance.

4

THE *FLYING ENTERPRISE,*
THE SS *BADGER STATE,*
AND THE *JOOLA*

Shipwrecks often leave survivors battling the elements for their very lives. For Captain Henrik Carlsen, an able seaman who had spent twenty-three of his thirty-seven years at sea, mere survival was not enough. The extent of his courage and dedication became known when his ship, the *Flying Enterprise*, was disabled and nearly destroyed at sea. Even as hurricane-force winds battered the *Flying Enterprise*, Captain Carlsen refused to abandon his ship.

HENRIK CARLSEN AND KENNETH DANCY ABOARD THE *FLYING ENTERPRISE*

The *Flying Enterprise*, an American freighter ship, departed Hamburg, Germany, for New York City on December 21, 1951, with a full cargo hold. Three days into the trip, the ship ran into one of the largest and most destructive Atlantic storms of the twentieth century. The ship battled the storm for three days. On

Captain Henrik Carlsen stands alone, holding on to a guardrail on the badly listing *Flying Enterprise.*

December 27, a tremendous wave struck the ship and cracked the hull. Carlsen put his crew to work filling the cracks with cement as a temporary repair. The next day, a 60-foot (18 m) wave smashed into the ship. The ship listed at a thirty-degree tilt, enough to flood the engines and make them inoperable.

Carlsen had the radio operator send out an SOS signal and gathered the crew and passengers on deck with their life vests. The *Flying Enterprise*'s lifeboats were unusable because of the ship's sharp list and the rough seas. When rescue ships appeared the next morning, Carlsen had the passengers and crew jump into the ocean to be picked up by rescuers. All but one crew member were successfully rescued. Carlsen himself remained on board the floundering ship, vowing to stay until it either made it into port or sank.

At that point, the *Flying Enterprise* was without heat, light, and electricity. Carlsen used flashlights to find his way around. With the radio inoperable, he used a battery-powered voice transmitter to communicate with other ships. The ship's sixty-degree list, combined with the storm, made walking on the decks difficult and dangerous. Carlsen was forced to crawl around on his hands and knees. The ship's bow was underwater and much of the hold was flooded.

He chose the radio operator's cabin as his headquarters, sleeping on a mattress wedged into a corner and keeping the door propped open so that he wouldn't be trapped if the ship started to sink. Wind and water constantly blew in through the open door. Captain Carlsen ate cake and fruit juice that he found in a storage room until one of the rescue ships managed to deliver supplies.

Help Arrives

Carlsen spent six days under those conditions before the storm blew itself out. Finally, on January 3, 1952, the British tugboat *Turmoil* arrived on the scene to pull the *Flying Enterprise* back to port. The sea was still too rough for the tugboat's crew to throw a line over to the *Flying Enterprise*. Instead, the *Turmoil's* captain got as close as possible to the ship and a sailor named Kenneth Dancy leaped aboard the *Flying Enterprise* to help secure a line. Dancy later marveled at Carlsen's calmness. While the captain had gotten used to living in the absurd conditions on board the ship, Dancy found it impossible to sleep at night with the ship shuddering as each wave struck.

For three days after Dancy's arrival, the *Turmoil* towed the *Flying Enterprise* toward the port of Falmouth, England. Then, on January 8, another storm came up. Carlsen and Darcy hung on as the ship pitched on the seas for five hours. That night, the two men were awakened by the *Turmoil*'s siren, signaling that the tow rope had broken. The next morning, the ship was hit by another monstrous wave that nearly swept Carlsen and Dancy into the sea. By January 10, the ship was taking in more water as the storm continued. Finally, with most of the ship underwater, they gave up and jumped into the ocean, where they were rescued by the *Turmoil*. Minutes later, the *Flying Enterprise* sank, just 41 miles (66 km) from Falmouth.

The world had remained riveted by Captain Carlsen's two-week ordeal aboard the *Flying Enterprise*. After their rescue, Carlsen and Dancy were hailed as heroes. Awards and honors were showered on "Stay Put Carlsen," and New York City treated him to a ticker-tape parade. Though he humbly accepted the honors, he steadfastly refused most interviews or offers to buy his story. Instead, Carlsen returned to the sea as quickly as possible, feeling that he had failed in his mission to bring the ship back to port.

THE SS *BADGER STATE*

The American Merchant Marine ship SS *Badger State*, a former naval ship owned by the State Marine Lines company, departed on

December 23, 1969, for Da Nang, Vietnam. The ship carried a crew of forty men and a shipment of nearly 2,000 pounds of explosives for use by the United States Air Force in the Vietnam War. It encountered a violent storm just three days after leaving port. As the ship tossed on the waves, some of the explosives in the hold broke free and began rolling around in the hull. On December 27, an explosion caused by the loose weaponry ripped the hull open.

Captain Charles Wilson

When the storm hit and the bombs in the hold broke free, Captain Charles Wilson had his men go down and brace them with planks. Repairs were made to a leak in the hull. He cut the boat's speed and turned it off course from Da Nang, heading for the port on Midway Island to have the cargo secured. Wilson stayed on the bridge day and night, trying to maintain a southerly course against the wind. The sea was too violent. Finally, on December 27, he acknowledged that the ship was doomed.

Even as he gave the order to slow the ship and bring the lifeboat down, a bomb exploded, tearing a hole in the ship. The captain and a small team of volunteers managed to lower the lifeboat with thirty-five men on board. The boat would try to make it to a nearby rescue ship, the *Khian Star*. Wilson and his volunteers had to take their chances in the icy water until they were rescued. Buoyed by his life vest and a life preserver, Wilson desperately swam toward the *Khian Star*, where he was safely pulled on board.

Jim Beattie

Among the men in the lifeboat was Jim Beattie. As one of the ship's three firemen, Beattie's duty was to tend to the *Badger State's* steam boilers. On board the lifeboat, Beattie watched in terror as waves pushed it toward a massive hole in the ship's hull. The ship itself shifted, and a bomb slid right into the lifeboat, flipping it over and tossing men into the sea.

Beattie swam for about a mile toward the *Khian Star*, but he misjudged the ship's position and was forced to swim back to the capsized lifeboat. As he neared it, an albatross landed on his head and started pecking at his face. Looking around, he could see the large sea birds attacking other survivors. Finally, a wave swept him close to the *Khian Star* and he was hauled on board by the crew. Of the *Badger State*'s forty-man crew, only fourteen survived the disaster.

The *Joola*

Today, safety measures and modern technology have reduced the incidence of catastrophe at sea. Still, hundreds of lives are lost each year when ferries meet with disaster, especially in the developing world. One such tragedy was the sinking of the Senegalese ferry *Joola* off of the coast of Gambia in 2002.

The *Joola* departed southern Senegal for the northern capital city of Dakar on September 26. Many of the passengers were women traveling to market and schoolchildren returning from summer vacation. One such student, Ben Bechir Badji, could see that the boat was severely overcrowded. Although the ferry was equipped to carry a maximum of 550 passengers, there were nearly 2,000 people on board.

At 11 PM, the ferry capsized in bad weather about 20 miles (32 km) from land. It overturned in a matter of minutes, trapping more than 1,000 people inside. Hundreds more were thrown into the water to be buffeted about by choppy water and high winds. Badji managed to cling to the upturned keel of the capsized boat until early morning. He was saved by Senegalese fishermen, many of whom risked their own lives to rescue the survivors. Sixty-four people survived the wreck of the *Joola*. More than 1,850 people died in the accident, the deadliest maritime disaster in African history.

The ordeals of shipwreck survivors illustrate how people faced with calamity can respond with feats of courage, endurance, and heroism. During centuries past, castaways survived long uncertain months of hunger and thirst. Shipwreck survivors from any time period have battled the same natural forces such as storms and ice.

Fishing boats and rescuers surround the capsized Senegalese ferry *Joola*, searching for survivors. In all, more people died in the shipwreck of the *Joola* than died when the *Titanic* sank, making it one of the worst maritime disasters of all time.

Today, modern communications, safety measures, and means of rescue cannot prevent fluke accidents and bad weather. However, such measures can increase the likelihood that disasters at sea will end in triumphant survivor stories, not tragedy.

GLOSSARY

albatross A large, web-footed sea bird found in the Southern Hemisphere and known for its powerful gliding flight.

blubber The insulating layer of fat found under the skin of whales and other large marine mammals.

brackish Somewhat salty.

cannibalism The practice of eating the flesh of one's own species.

capsize To flip over accidentally.

current A steady flow or movement in a definite direction.

deck A floorlike platform built on a sea vessel.

ferry A boat that transports people across water between two points on a regular schedule.

first mate On commercial ships, the officer's rank just below captain.

flotilla A fleet of small sea vessels.

frostbite The damage or destruction of living tissue by freezing, caused by low temperatures and exposure to the elements.

galley On a ship, the area where food is prepared.

harpoon A long-shafted, barbed spear attached to a strong line that is used for catching whales and large fish.

hull The frame or body of a ship.

list To tilt to one side.

magnate A wealthy and powerful businessperson.

mast On ships, a vertical beam used to support sails.

ocean liner A large commercial ship, usually one that carries passengers on long voyages and travels on a regular schedule.

pack ice A large expanse of floating sea ice.

ration To divide supplies into fixed portions for day-by-day use.

rudder A nautical steering device consisting of a hinged vertical plate set at a boat's stern.

second mate On commercial ships, the rank just below first mate.

stern The rear part of a ship.

tiller A lever used to turn a boat's rudder.

towline A strong line used to haul heavy materials.

FOR MORE INFORMATION

Great Lakes Shipwreck Museum

18335 N. Whitefish Point Road

Paradise, MI 49768

(888) 492-3747

Web site: http://www.shipwreckmuseum.com

National Maritime Historical Society

5 John Walsh Boulevard

P.O. Box 68

Peekskill, NY 10566

(800) 221-6647

Web site: http://www.seahistory.org

Naval Historical Center

Washington Navy Yard

805 Kidder Breese Street SE

Washington Navy Yard, DC 20374-5060

(202) 433-7880

Web site: http://www.history.navy.mil

Northern Maritime Research

P.O. Box 48047

Bedford, NS B4A 3Z2

Canada

(902) 445-5497

Web site: http://www.northernmaritimeresearch.com

United States Coast Guard

Coast Guard Headquarters

Commandant, U.S. Coast Guard

2100 Second Street SW

Washington, DC 20593

(206) 267-1587

Web site: http://www.uscg.mil/

WEB SITES

Due to the changing nature of Internet links, Rosen Publishing has developed an online list of Web sites related to the subject of this book. This site is updated regularly. Please use this link to access the list:

http://www.rosenlinks.com/ss/ship

FOR FURTHER READING

Armstrong, Jennifer. *Shipwreck at the Bottom of the World: The Extraordinary True Story of Shackleton and the* Endurance. New York, NY: Crown Books for Young Readers, 2000.

Ballard, Robert B. *Ghost Liners: Exploring the World's Greatest Lost Ships.* Boston, MA: Little, Brown, 1998.

Konstam, Angus. *The History of Shipwrecks.* Guilford, CT: Lyons Press, 2002.

Mayell, Hillary. *Shipwrecks.* San Diego, CA: Lucent Books, 2004.

Pellegrino, Charles R. *Ghosts of the* Titanic. New York, NY: William Morrow, 2000.

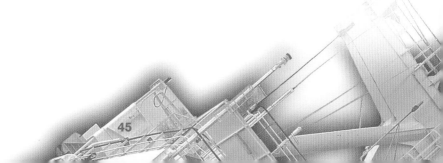

BIBLIOGRAPHY

BBC. "Senegal Ferry Survivors' Ordeal." September 30, 2002. Retrieved May 3, 2006 (http://news.bbc.co.uk/2/hi/africa/2288376.stm).

Benedetto, William R. *Sailing into the Abyss: A True Story of Extreme Heroism on the High Seas.* New York, NY: Citadel Press, 2005.

Butler, Hal. *Abandon Ship!* Chicago, IL: Henry Regnery Company, 1974.

Kamler, Kenneth, M.D. *Surviving the Extremes: A Doctor's Journey to the Limits of Human Endurance.* New York, NY: St. Martin's Press, 2004.

Lansing, Alfred. *Endurance: Shackleton's Incredible Voyage.* New York, NY: Carroll and Graf Publishers, Inc., 1999.

Lord, Walter. *A Night to Remember.* New York, NY: Bantam Books, 1988.

Maddocks, Melvin, and the editors of Time-Life Books. *The Great Liners* (The Seafarers). Alexandria, VA: Time-Life Books, 1978.

Philbrick, Nathaniel. *In the Heart of the Sea: The Tragedy of the Whaleship* Essex. New York, NY: Penguin Books, 2001.

Shackleton, Ernest. *South.* New York, NY: Carroll and Graf Publishers, Inc., 1998.

Tibballs, Geoff, ed. *The Mammoth Book of the* Titanic*: Contemporary Accounts from Survivors and the World's Press.* New York, NY: Carroll and Graf Publishers, Inc., 2002.

INDEX

ABOUT THE AUTHOR

Jason Porterfield is a writer and researcher who lives in Chicago, Illinois.

PHOTO CREDITS

Cover © Louise Gubb/Corbis; p. 4 © Jon Sparks/Corbis; p. 6 Rare Books Division, The New York Public Library, Astor, Lenox and Tilden Foundations; p. 9 © Edward Gooch/Getty Images; pp. 10, 14 Courtesy of the Nantucket Historical Association; p. 17 © Central Press/Getty Images; p. 20 © Mary Evans Picture Library/The Image Works; pp. 22, 23 © Ralph White/Corbis; p. 27 © Mansell/Mansell/Time & Life Pictures/Getty Images; p. 30 Scott Polar Research Institute; p. 31 © Topical Press Agency/Getty Images; p. 34 ©Bettmann/Corbis; p. 40 © AFP/Getty Images.

Designer: Tahara Anderson; Editor: Wayne Anderson
Photo Researcher: Amy Feinberg